CLUB 75

The Troub Abracadab

Alan Plater

M

Macmillan Education

First published 1975

Published by
MACMILLAN EDUCATION LTD
London and Basingstoke
Associated companies and representatives throughout the world
Filmset by BAS Printers Limited, Wallop, Hampshire
Printed in Great Britain by
Ebenezer Baylis & Son Ltd
The Trinity Press, Leicester and London

Illustrator: Trevor Stubley

CONTENTS

1 Funny walks

There's nothing like watching the big ships come in on the tide. If you live by a river, it's the best free show in town; and if you live inland, that's your hard luck.

Ted lives near enough to a river. So every free night when it isn't raining, he's down by the lock gates, watching the big ships, and the little ones as well. A hundred years ago there were whalers, battered by the Arctic storms – or so his dad says – but now everything's modern: container ships with everything pre-packed in these big sort of tins. Everything's in tins these days, according to Ted's dad, unless it's deep-frozen. Very often it's both.

Anyhow, Ted's down there this night, standing and staring along with the usual mixed crowd. There's a few kids more or less his own age, which is twelve, a handful of dockers going on or off shift, foreign seamen togged up to enjoy the city's night life – mugs, according to Ted's dad, and the old men.

Funny. Whenever there's anything to watch – the ships locking in, a hole in the road, the ducks on the park pond – there'll be old men watching. They never say much but you can tell what they're

thinking. They're thinking they'd be fifty times better at doing the job – skippering the ship, digging the hole, looking after the ducks – if anybody asked them to do it. But nobody ever does.

Nobody ever asks them to do funny walks either, but tonight one of the old men is doing a funny walk. Sometimes they walk badly but that's usually on account of old age or bad legs or rheumatism and that's not very funny. But this night, as the ship was nosing its way through the lock gates, Ted found himself watching an old man.

He was just walking up and down, ten paces there,

ten paces back. Ted counted them. Turning at the far end of his walk, the old man saw Ted watching, and smiled. Ted smiled back, being a friendly sort of kid. Then the old man carried on walking, stiff-legged, toes pointing out, a bit like Charlie Chaplin, and you couldn't help laughing – well, smiling, anyway. And then he fell over.

Except that he didn't. What he did was stumble, hover in mid-air for a split-second that seemed longer, then recover his balance. Ted had already taken a couple of paces towards him to help him up again – but there was no point, because he wasn't down. So Ted looked around to see what the old man had tripped over, expecting to find a piece of rope, a length of rusty chain or maybe an old railway sleeper. There was nothing. He had tripped over something that wasn't there.

Ted was impressed. Anybody can trip over something that's there, but it takes talent to trip over something that isn't there. All the same, he decided to check.

'Are you all right, Mister?'

The old man smiled a beaming smile, though it might have beamed brighter if he'd had better teeth and more of them.

'I'm in excellent health and spirits, my boy – it's the others.'

He had a funny voice: ordinary but trying to be posh, like Ted's teacher, Miss Chapman. She had quite a posh voice all the time, without trying too hard, but one day when an Inspector came into the classroom, her voice changed. Not that she *spoke* any posher: more like she was trying to say the right things and think posh thoughts. You've got to do that with Inspectors, probably.

The ship was through the lock gates now, heading downriver, and the spectators drifting away on their own tide. On their way to home, night shift, beer, fish and chips, rows for being late, show-jumping on the telly or what Miss Chapman called 'creative hobbies'. Ted knew a man in their street who was making the *Flying Scotsman* out of used match-sticks but didn't like to ask him why.

As they wandered towards the dock exit Ted walked not exactly with the old man, but near enough to hear what he said if he decided to talk again. After about twenty metres of nothing happening, Ted decided to leap in. If in doubt, lash out, his dad always said.

'Do you do anything else,' said Ted, 'apart from not falling over?'

'I'm glad you asked me that,' said the old man, obviously happy with the question. 'I'm a dream-

weaver, a dealer in magic and spells, a provoker of mirth and merriment. My card.'

He held out a small, rectangular, dog-eared business card with some writing on. Ted glimpsed some faded gilt words '. . . AVAILABLE PANTOMIME, SUMMER SEASONS AND . . .' but as he took hold of the card, it disappeared. Ted was certain he'd touched the card, held it, even. Then there it was, gone. Like his dad said about his last pay rise: now you see it, now you don't.

Ted had never met a magical man face to face. At least, he'd never met one who owned up.

'Can anybody learn it?' he said.

'I can teach people to trip over invisible obstacles, perform amusing feats. Impress your friends. Win many cigars.'

So there and then the lessons began. In the silent acres of dockland, the old man taught Ted how to fall over invisible obstacles. And he threw in funny walks for good measure.

'Remember that funny walks are mostly animal walks. There's the chicken walk . . . all jerky, like that . . . knees stiff, stick your bottom out, elbows up. Use your head, remember you've got a beak, you're looking for things to peck . . .'

A local citizen, riding past on his bike, almost fell off because he wasn't used to seeing people walking around like chickens on the docks at that time in the evening. The old man took no notice. He was in his own world.

'Now penguins, they're very interesting. They walk as if they're imitating people. So if we walk like penguins, we're really walking like people but the way penguins see us. Fascinating, don't you agree, my boy?'

They walked like penguins towards the dock gates. Ted could see a policeman standing there, a tall man with a thin black moustache, as if he'd been drinking tar, and Ted wasn't sure how he'd feel about penguin walks.

As they approached the policeman the old man stopped his penguin waddle and walked in a normal but dignified way. He raised one hand in greeting to the policeman – like the Queen waving from her Rolls-Royce – and with his other hand raised his battered trilby hat, which looked as though it had been to the Arctic with the whalers.

'Good evening, constable,' he said, 'May God bless you and your colleagues who keep the streets safe for the elderly.'

'Keep moving,' said the policeman.

'Good advice,' replied the old man. 'Keep moving, present a more difficult target to the enemy.'

They walked on quickly, as the policeman's moustache seemed on the brink of bristling. Beyond the gate, Ted turned left and the old man right.

Before they parted, Ted asked him:

'Can you teach me any more funny walks and things?'

'And much more besides. Even a little wisdom, if you're interested. Most people think it all very strange these days.'

'I don't think it's strange.'

'There are very few of us left, my boy.'

So saying, and looking a little sad, the old man raised his hat, gave a slight bow and walked off into the dockland dusk, as if he was leaving the stage at the end of a performance.

Ted was late home and they sent him straight to bed: school in the morning, all the usual stuff. As he crossed the living room, he did a chicken walk, tripped over an invisible obstacle without actually falling, did a quick bow and went out of the room.

'Have to get that carpet fixed,' said his dad.

2 The Palace ruins

Miss Chapman looked at the class with her best I'm-Going-To-Say-Something-Important expression. Then she said it.

'William Shakespeare was one of the greatest men who ever lived. Let's write his name down, shall we?'

Ted yawned. Mike, sitting next to him, didn't yawn, but was obviously thinking a yawn. It was a yawning hot day and the school had glass where you'd expect walls to be, and the odd chunk of brickwork where you might expect a window. Great for tomatoes, Ted reckoned.

Miss Chapman wrote on the blackboard: WILLIAM SHAKESPEARE 1564–1616. Thirty-six hands wrote in thirty-six exercise books: WILLIAM SHAKESPEARE 1564–1616. The writing wasn't as neat as Miss Chapman's, except for Deidre Hardaker's, but she was a doctor's daughter.

'Now,' said Miss Chapman, with a business-like clap of the hands, 'Shakespeare's most famous play was *Hamlet*. Hands up anybody who's heard of *Hamlet* . . .'

A few hands went halfway up, mostly kids wanting to impress without being put to the test. But not Ted. His hand shot right up, straight and bold. Miss Chapman was pleased.

'Yes, Ted. What can you tell us about *Hamlet*?'

'Please miss, it's a kind of cigar.'

The class laughed, a bit loud and raucous, considering it wasn't all that funny. But it was near the end of the afternoon and everybody was hot, sweaty, fed up and ready for off. Miss Chapman must have been fed up as well because she didn't laugh at all.

She droned on about how silly it was to make jokes, especially silly jokes. Then before long she was reciting . . .

'To be or not to be,
That is the question . . .'

But nobody listened. Mike whispered to Ted.

'Playing football tonight after?'

'No,' said Ted.

'Where you going?' said Mike.

'Secret,' said Ted.

'Tell us.'

Ted hesitated. He knew it might sound daft. But he also knew Mike was very persistent. So he told him.

'I'm off to see the Palace ruins.'

'What Palace ruins?'

'Secret. Dead secret.'

It had to be dead secret, because Ted didn't know himself. The old man said: meet me near Harrison's salerooms and I'll show you the Palace ruins.

Ted was saved by the school bell from Mike, and from Shakespeare. He ran out of school and kept on running until he arrived at Harrison's, where once a week there were auction sales of assorted choice items. Ted's dad used to go to the sales, picking up bargains, he said, until his mam said she didn't want any more bird cages or stuffed squirrels in glass cases.

The old man wasn't there. Ted hung around for a few minutes, nearly got run over by two men carrying a sideboard, then set off walking past buildings being knocked down ready for improvements that hadn't happened yet.

It was on one of these flat, vacant sites that Ted saw the old man, standing, surrounded by broken

bricks and bottles, with weeds and nettles growing round stumps of old walls. If you needed a dead cat in a hurry, this was the sort of place you'd look.

'Sorry I'm late,' said Ted. 'We were doing Shakespeare.'

'Ah, Shakespeare,' said the old man, 'the noblest performer of them all.'

He was gazing around at the wild flowers, the broken glass, the rusty bed-springs. Ted asked the question.

'What about the Palace ruins?'

'These *are* the Palace ruins. Here, on this very spot, there stood a great, glittering Palace, built of fine stone, quarried and carved with loving skill. And in the Palace dwelt jugglers and fire-eaters, lion tamers and sword swallowers, trick cyclists and sand-dancers. Tellers of tales and singers of songs.'

'Here,' said Ted.

'Here. And look what the vandals did.'

Ted was puzzled. Vandals usually wrote on walls or broke windows, which seemed a bit daft. But knocking down a whole building was a fair achievement. The old man seemed to read his mind.

'Not childish vandals. Grown-up vandals. The ones we vote for. They took my Palace and they destroyed it. They said they had good reasons, but look at it . . .'

The old man looked at the wasteland, and sighed at the memory. Ted decided he'd try to cheer him up, so he told him about the joke he'd made in class, about Hamlet and the cigar. The old man smiled and seemed pleased.

'Mind you,' he said, 'I can give you some better jokes for next time.'

Next day, in class, Miss Chapman started on about Shakespeare again, to see whether they'd been listening the previous afternoon.

'Now then,' she said brightly, 'Who can tell me who wrote *Hamlet*?'

Ted's hand shot up, the first and the quickest.

'Please, Miss, it wasn't me.'

Everybody laughed, except Miss Chapman, but she tried to ignore Ted.

'What else can anybody tell me about Shakespeare?'

Again Ted was the first to react.

'Please, Miss, he's dead. All the great people are dead. Shakespeare's dead, Beethoven's dead, Rembrandt's dead. And I don't feel so well myself.'

After three more of the old man's jokes, Miss Chapman sent Ted to see the headmaster, Mr Earnshaw, a big brawny man with a laugh like a second-hand car refusing to start. Ted explained he'd been making jokes in class. Mr Earnshaw asked him to repeat the jokes. He listened, like a man trying hard not to laugh, then put on a very serious face.

'Obviously I'll have to tan your backside.'

This puzzled Ted because Mr Earnshaw never used a cane.

'And you know what that will mean? If I give you six of the best?'

'No, sir.'

'It means I shall get you in the end.'

Ted looked hard at Mr Earnshaw. Neither of them laughed. But Ted was sure that Mr Earnshaw had once visited the Palace ruins, probably before the vandals moved in.

3 Walk through the Paradise Gardens

All down the long days of summer, Ted and the old man explored the city, seeking out the lost and golden palaces.

They visited the Mechanic's Institute that became Springthorpe's that became Messrs Bosco and Downs' Empire Music Hall. They gazed at the Alhambra that became the Hippodrome. They queued for the cheap gallery seats at the Royal Queen's Theatre, part of which became the New Theatre Royal, which became the Tivoli Music Hall. They stared in awe at the waxworks and at Hengler's celebrated circus.

All gone, of course, but the old man made them live again for Ted. Acrobats tumbled, magicians astounded them before their very eyes. Ted even found out the old man's name.

'My boy, I am called Dan, after Dan Leno, the greatest funny man of our time.'

'Is he still alive?'

'Good Heavens, no. He died over seventy years ago.'

'I don't feel so well myself,' said Ted, but Dan was staring at the glass-fronted office block that stood where once there'd been the Tivoli, the 'fishermen's theatre'.

'Why did they get rid of the halls?' asked Ted.

'It would appear,' said Dan, a little pompously, 'that the world prefers office blocks and motor cars to laughter.'

'That's daft.'

'Yes,' said Dan.

The stories tumbled out of Dan. Tales of Charlie Chaplin and Stan Laurel who were famous Hollywood film stars but first learned to make people laugh working on the music hall stages for a man called Fred Karno. Karno ran troupes of knockabout comedians and tumblers.

'My Dad says he works for Fred Karno . . . a real Fred Karno outfit he calls it,' said Ted.

'All part of history, my boy. Like Tich.'

'Tich? We've got a kid in our class we call Tich. He's only little.'

Dan smiled.

'I'll tell you why you call him Tich.'

And he told Ted about the greatest Tich of them all: Little Tich. He was a comedian, only five feet tall, who wore enormous boots and did strange, hilarious dances. His real name was Harry Relph and the first time he appeared on the stage he played the penny whistle. There was a twenty-stone man called Titchborne appearing the same night and the theatre manager had said:

'We've got Big Titch appearing tonight . . . let's have Little Tich as well.'

So Ted discovered the reason that small people are called Tich. But he still didn't learn very much about Dan.

He tried again one day as they were walking in the gardens in the centre of the city – gardens that had once been a dock filled with sailing ships, and you could still see a piece of the old dock wall.

'Do you ever do funny walks for a living?'

'Look,' said Dan, and Ted knew he was changing the subject.

And, as usual, he changed the subject beautifully. He rummaged around in a waste-bin, and brought out two empty lemonade cans and an old beer bottle. He threw each one up in the air and caught it as it came down, trying them for size and weight. Then he juggled with them, just simple juggling at first: that's to say, he made it *look* simple.

There were variations as he threw cans or bottle up behind his back or through his legs, or all three extra-high, doing a complete turn round, clapping his hands, arriving back face-to-front, just in time to catch them.

He caught the three, one at a time, gave a big smile and bowed to Ted. Ted clapped him. He knew by now exactly when Dan expected applause. The funny thing was, Ted could hear somebody else clapping as well.

First he saw the long shadow on the grass and then, standing at the end of the shadow, he saw the policeman. The thin black moustache was familiar.

'What do you think you're up to?' said the man in dark blue.

'I'm up to the juggling,' said Dan. 'Next I shall dive from a hundred-foot tower into a wet flannel.'

'Ha ha,' said the policeman but it wasn't a real laugh from the heart. 'Supposing I decide you're causing a breach of the peace and give you a smart kick in the pants?'

'You'll get him in the end,' said Ted.

This did not please the policeman but before he could say or do anything, Dan walked up to him.

'I think I can help you, officer. Make your life a happier experience.'

Dan raised his hand and took an egg from the policeman's left ear. Then, with the other hand, he took a second egg from the policeman's right ear.

'There,' said Dan. 'You'll be able to see much better now.'

Dan and Ted walked away. The policeman started to take out his notebook.

'I think it's the same policeman we saw at the docks,' said Ted.

'They all look alike to the poor and dispossessed,' said Dan, and again Ted wasn't sure what he meant.

When they were a safe distance away from the Law, Dan threw the two eggs high in the air where they disappeared.

The following evening, Ted's dad announced that he 'wanted a word' with him. Ted was in the shed looking for an old tin tray when his dad came in and said it:

'I want a word with you.'

'Which word did you want, Dad?' replied Ted, and then ducked as Dad threw a fast, friendly left hook at his chin. He'd been a boxer once, in the Army, but he'd taught Ted how to bob and weave and protect his chin.

'We had the police round,' said Dad. 'They say you're keeping bad company.'

'Who do they mean? Mike?'

Mike had been up in the Juvenile Court once for trespassing on railway property but they'd just given him a telling-off.

'Something about an old man. Hanging round town with an old man.'

'Not me. Must have been two other fellers.'

'Just be careful, that's all.'

'I'll be all right, Dad,' Ted said. 'You taught me to keep my guard up and protect my chin.'

Next day, Ted told Dan what had happened.

'I'm not supposed to see you. The police say you're bad company.'

'The police are right,' said Dan. 'I *am* bad company. In my time I have drunk beer, played the tables, backed horses. I sometimes tell lies. I occasionally spend money that I don't possess.'

'That doesn't seem all that terrible.'

'But I have also sat with the Gods,' said Dan.

Again, Ted wasn't quite sure what the old man meant. But it sounded good and Ted had discovered that sometimes you could have more fun if you didn't do as you were told. As long as you kept your guard up to protect your chin.

4 Tea at the Royal

Ted's mother looked puzzled. Not just puzzled but gob-smacked, to use one of his dad's favourite words, except she didn't like him to use it, especially in company. But that is what she looked.

'You want *what*?' she said to Ted.

'Five teaspoons, five cups and a tray.'

'What do you want them for?'

Ted explained that you glued the cups to the tray, in a row, then lined the spoons up, one in front of each cup, picked up the tray carefully, then gave a quick jerk, throwing the spoons up in the air and catching them as they fell – one spoon in each cup.

His mother said it would be a better idea if he got to bed earlier and maybe she'd get him a tonic from the chemists, because obviously he was run down. Probably the warm weather was affecting his brain.

'Why don't you go out and play with Mike?'

'Yes. All right.'

Out he went, but not to play with Mike. He'd already arranged to meet Dan and they were taking a trip to the cemetery. 'Bring your friends,' the old man had said.

'What you want to go to the cemetery for?' Mike

had said when Ted suggested it. Ted couldn't tell him, because he didn't really know.

It was a long, long walk to the cemetery, and it was in the middle of a housing estate that they found it. Dan led the way in, and he knew exactly where to go.

He stopped beside a small, grey headstone.

'Read that,' he said.

Ted read the inscription.

'Arthur Lucan. Better known and beloved by all children as Old Mother Riley.

Don't cry as you pass by,
Just say a little prayer.'

'Old Mother Riley,' said Ted, 'I saw an Old Mother Riley film on the telly.'

'Now you know why we came here,' said Dan. 'To pay homage to a great comedian. He died in work, collapsed on stage at the old Tivoli. Nearly twenty years ago. That's the way to go, working to the end.'

There were fresh flowers on the grave.

'You see?' said the old man, pointing to the flowers. 'Somebody still remembers.'

They stood there for quite a long time and Ted was beginning to fidget, without being disrespectful.

'Always the best way, to go while you're working. Like Chung Ling Soo.'

'Who?'

'Chung Ling Soo. Amazing Chinese Magician. His real name was Will Robinson. His greatest trick was to stand on one side of the stage while his assistant fired a revolver at him and he would catch the bullet in his teeth. Then one night the trick didn't work.'

'Did it kill him?'

'Bullets usually do.'

Ted was beginning to wonder when all this gloomy talk was going to end. He soon discovered the answer – not yet.

'Oh yes, they've all gone. Marie Lloyd, Gus Elen, Randolph Sutton, Dan Leno . . .'

'Did they all shoot themselves?' asked Ted.

'No. Just natural causes. I mean, if Dan Leno was alive today, he'd be coming up to his one-hundred-and-fourteenth birthday.'

'So many wrinkles on his forehead, he has to screw his hat on,' said Ted, repeating a line Dan had taught him.

For the first time that afternoon, the old man smiled. Not just a smile, but a laugh.

'Good boy. Here I am getting all morbid and you've reminded me that where there's life there's hope. I know. Let's take tea in style.'

'We haven't got any money.'

'But I have a great deal of influence in this city,' announced Dan.

They walked the long road back to the city centre and Ted wondered why it was that Dan had no influence with bus conductors.

But walk they did, right into the heart of the city, up the steps and through the swing doors of the Royal Hotel. The Royal was so posh that First Division football teams stayed there when they were playing cup ties against the local club.

'We haven't got any money,' Ted repeated as Dan led him into a large room with big, deep armchairs, round polished tables, and a carpet that felt like you were paddling in shallow water at Bridlington.

They sat down and Dan beckoned to a waiter.

'A pot of tea in a silver teapot for myself, a large lemonade for my young friend and half-a-hundred-weight of your finest cream cakes which we will share.'

The tea and the lemonade and the cakes arrived and Ted was still overwhelmed by the surroundings and worried about how they were going to pay. But the taste of the first cream cake eased his mind. After the fourth, he decided to stop for decency's sake. He sat back in the chair, very contented.

'Now off you go,' said Dan.

'Are you coming?'

'In the fullness of time, my boy. I have to meet somebody. A business appointment. I do most of my business here at the Royal.'

Ted did as he was told. He walked through the

ROYAL HOTEL
HOTEL
ROYAL HOTEL

swing doors and out into the noise and petrol fumes of the city centre. As he turned at the end of the road, he saw a police car driving into the hotel forecourt. Must have been an accident, he decided.

His dad was surprised to hear that he'd been to the cemetery, and pleased as well, because he was able to repeat his favourite joke.

'The cemetery? That's the dead centre of the city.'

But Ted was already on his way out to the shed. He'd found some plastic beakers under the sink, left over from Christmas, and he'd borrowed five spoons from the kitchen drawer.

In the shed was a piece of hardboard that would serve as a tray. Ted fastened the plastic beakers to his makeshift tray with drawing pins and only pierced his finger once. Then he took tray, cups and spoons out into the backyard. You needed space for a job like this.

He lined up the spoons, one in front of each cup. He cried out the magic word.

'Abracadabra!'

He threw the spoons up in the air and they dropped all over the yard.

'What are you doing?' said his dad, through the open kitchen window, shaving himself, ready for his darts night.

'Dropping spoons,' said Ted.

'Thought so.'

Dad closed the window and got on with his shave. Ted shrugged his shoulders. Like Dan had once said to him: there'll always be some people who don't understand what you mean by Abracadabra.

5 Curtain call

After they had taken tea in the Royal Hotel, Ted didn't see old Dan for weeks on end. He went to the usual places: the dockside at high tide, the Palace ruins and one day he even went to the cemetery, in the rain. He put three flowers on Old Mother Riley's grave, first making sure that nobody was looking. He had to do that because he took the flowers off another grave.

Then school started again, after the holiday, and their new teacher, Mr Bradley, was straight out of college and very enthusiastic about new ideas.

'We'll have to do something about him, he's too keen,' said Mike, but they couldn't think of anything to do.

Mr Bradley believed in taking the class out of school on educational visits. They all went to the fish dock, to the brewery, and to a factory that made face cream. It was all called social studies but Ted wasn't sure why, except that they usually had a few laughs on the way there and back, and that was a bit social.

One day towards the end of October, Mr Bradley took them on a visit to the Magistrates' Court. Ted and Mike sat upstairs on the bus, at the front, pretending to be astronauts Armstrong and Aldrin, until Mr Bradley told them to be their age. They spent the rest of the journey pretending to be Tom and Jerry.

The courtroom was in a big, ornamental, stone building, like an old grey wedding cake. They went through a large doorway, up some stairs, along a corridor, up some more stairs, along another corridor. Big Eddie said they'd come in the wrong door in the first place. He knew that because he'd been to the court before, when his brother was up for stealing lead. Mr Bradley didn't want to talk about Eddie's brother.

One staircase and two corridors later, they found the place they were looking for, and all filed into the visitors' gallery at the court. Mr Bradley had explained to them the day before what the system was. There were the magistrates sitting on the bench. ('They're like the referees,' said Ted) and a Clerk of the Court who explained the rules to everybody. There was a Prosecuting Counsel to say what it was the man had done. There was a Defending Counsel to say hang on a minute, he didn't do it.

They arrived just as a man was being fined twenty-five pounds for a driving offence and he seemed most unhappy about it. Then a voice said 'Next case' and into the dock walked Old Dan. Ted stared, and tried to attract Dan's attention, but he was facing the other way.

The first witness appeared and he turned out to be the policeman with the thin, black moustache.

He muttered a few words that Ted couldn't hear properly and then the magistrate in the middle said something about 'remanded in custody pending further inquiries'.

'What's custody?' said Mike.

'Prison,' said Ted.

Then Dan, in a very loud voice, said 'Thank you, my man.' Ted remembered what Dan had told him:

'You've got to make your voice heard in the back row of the Gods.'

Then the incident happened. As Dan left the dock, he walked across to the Clerk of the Court, stopped and took an egg from each of the man's ears.

There was a shocked silence, as if nobody could believe it, then Ted laughed out loud. Mike laughed and Big Eddie – who had the biggest guffaw in the class – joined in. All the class laughed. The policeman smiled. The magistrates and the Clerk of the Court did not laugh, and the magistrate in the middle said:

'If visitors cannot behave in a seemly manner, I shall have to ask them to leave.'

Old Dan made his way out of the court room.

‘Back to the dungeons,’ said Mike.

Just as he reached the door, Ted, without thinking what he was doing, let out a loud clucking noise, exactly like a hen that has just laid an egg. It was exactly as the old man had taught him.

Dan looked up at Ted, saw him, and winked at him. All the class laughed and again the Boss Magistrate told them to be quiet.

Mr Bradley was very annoyed about the way the class had behaved. He had planned to take them to a great cathedral but now he wasn’t so sure they deserved it. They all pretended to be disappointed.

It was a month later that Ted’s dad showed him the item in the local paper. It said that Dan had been sent to prison for six months.

‘It was stated that the accused made a habit of running up large bills at various shops and hotels, only to leave without paying. If approached, he would pay with a cheque that subsequently turned out to be worthless.

‘He also used a variety of false names, including Daniel Leno, Stanley Laurel and William Robinson.’

‘Same as Chung Ling Soo,’ said Ted to his dad.

Dad looked at the paper, then at Ted.

‘You’re as mad as him.’

Then Ted saw the best bit in the newspaper report.

‘There was an incident as “Robinson” left the court. He approached the chief police witness for the prosecution and apparently removed an egg from each of his ears. He then threw the eggs into the air

where they disappeared, before he was restrained by several police officers.'

Ted showed this paragraph to his dad.

'Why would he take eggs from someone's ears?' his dad asked.

'To help him to see better,' Ted replied, then ducked as Dad threw a swift right-cross.

Ted ducked into the back yard. It was sad about Dan, but Ted was sure the old man would be able to cope with prison. Or any other place, for that matter.

In the shed, Ted dug out the tray with the cups fastened to it, and the spoons. His mother was still wondering about those spoons.

But now the job was the only thing that mattered. He set out the spoons on the tray, one in front of each cup. He said the magic word.

'Abracadabra!'

He tossed the spoons in the air and they scattered all over the back yard. Ted picked them up, and again he set them out on the tray. Once more he said the magic word.

'Abracadabra!'

He tossed the spoons in the air and they scattered all over the back yard.

Ted found a piece of chalk and kept the score on the back yard wall. In that way, he knew it was his nineteenth attempt when the five spoons landed in the five cups, one to each cup.

Ted took the triumph very quietly.

'Right,' he said to nobody in particular, apart from himself. 'That proves that *I* understand what abracadabra means, even if nobody else does.'

Then he went off to play football with Mike.